Madame Pantomime's

Balinese Dream

Flora and Fauna Textile Designs

An Adult Coloring Book

The Dragons Say:

"Don't forget to use a bleeder page!"

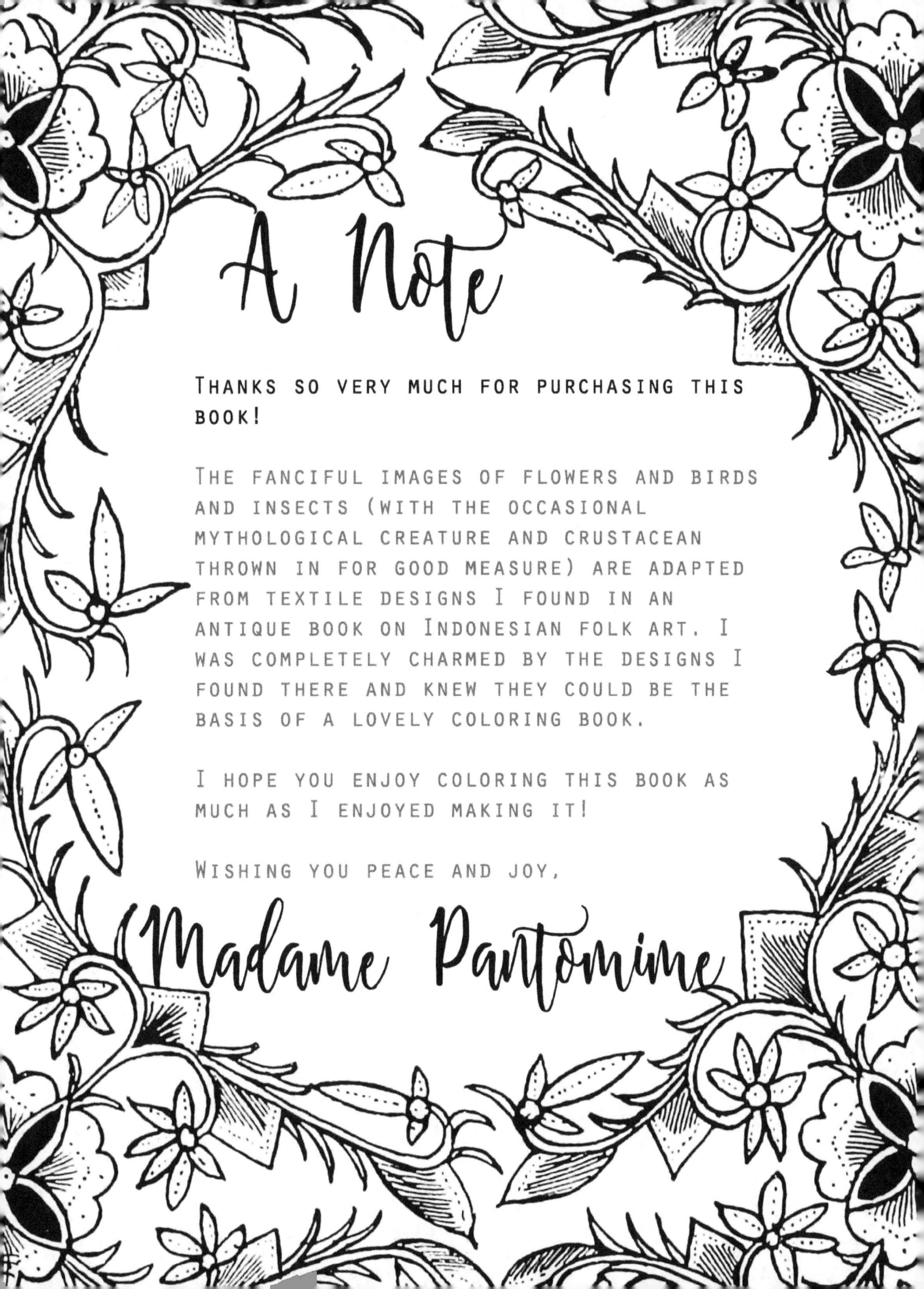

A Note

Thanks so very much for purchasing this book!

The fanciful images of flowers and birds and insects (with the occasional mythological creature and crustacean thrown in for good measure) are adapted from textile designs I found in an antique book on Indonesian folk art. I was completely charmed by the designs I found there and knew they could be the basis of a lovely coloring book.

I hope you enjoy coloring this book as much as I enjoyed making it!

Wishing you peace and joy,

Madame Pantomime

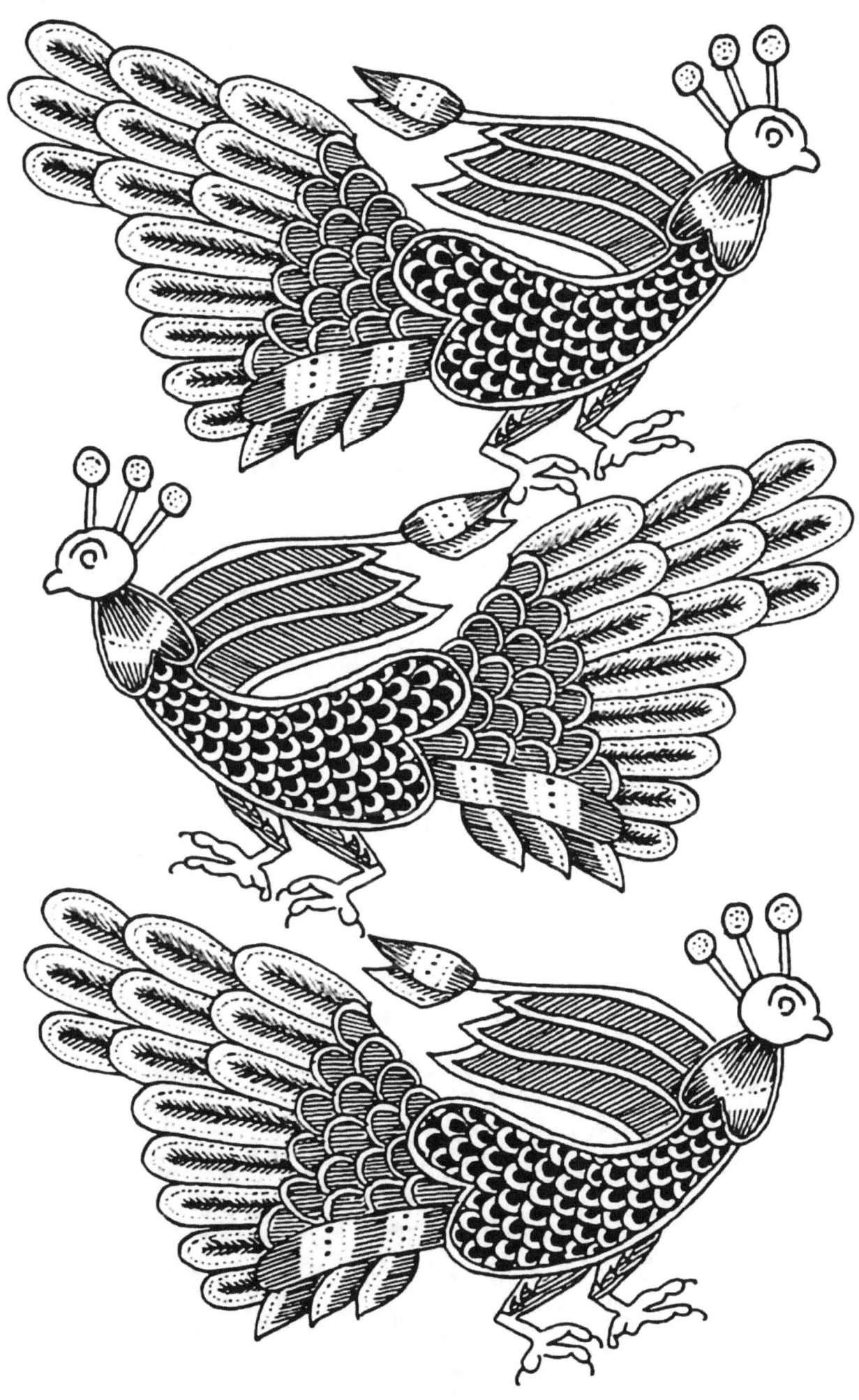

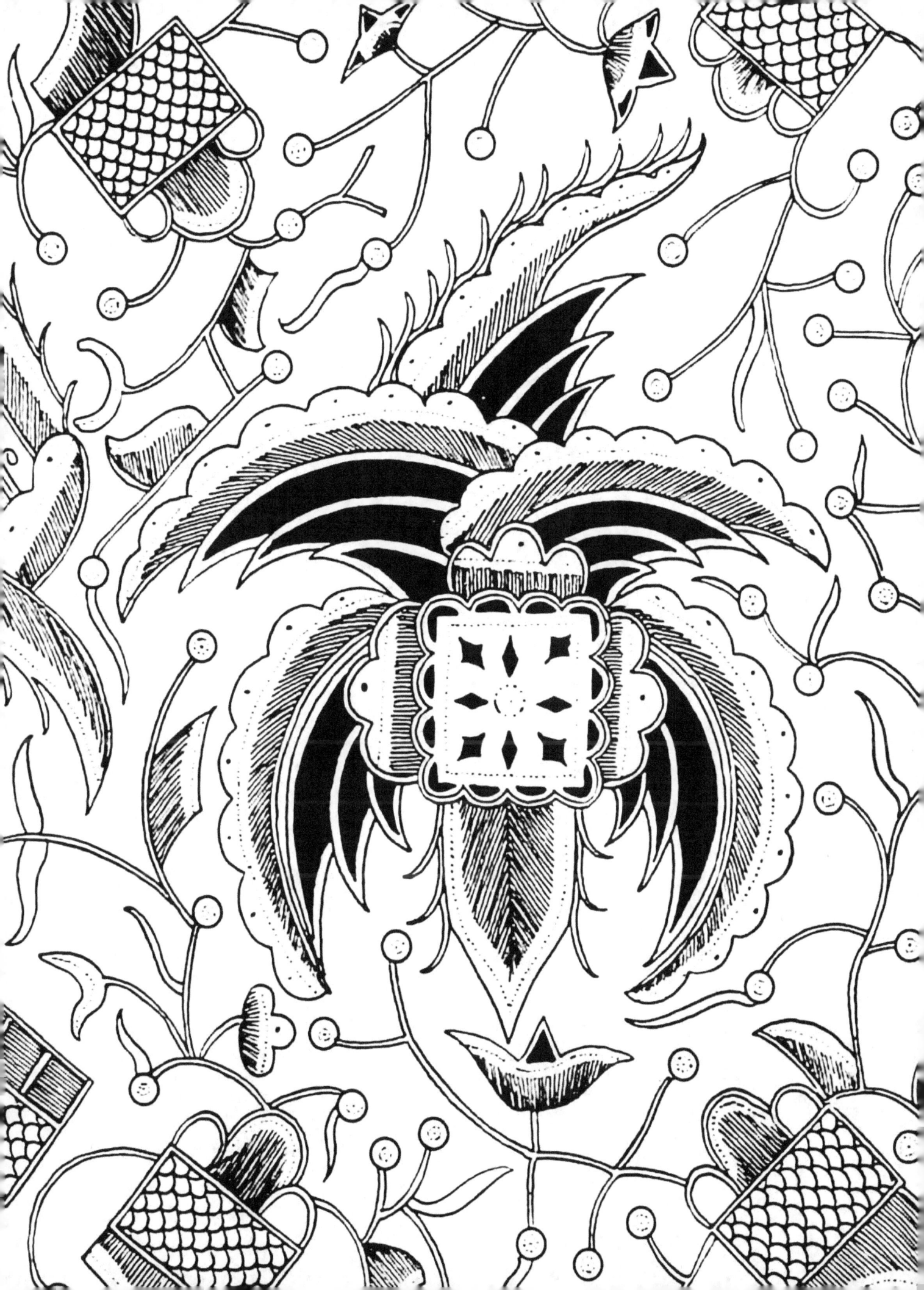

If you enjoyed this coloring book, you might also like my Indonesian Textile Design-Inspired Coloring Book Journal, Balinese Journey.

On the next three pages I've Included Three Bonus Images From this Coloring Book Journal.

If you'd Like to purchase your very own Copy of Balinese Journey, It's available from Amazon, or if you'd like to print your own at home, you can find the printable version at: WWW.MADAMEPANTOMIME.COM

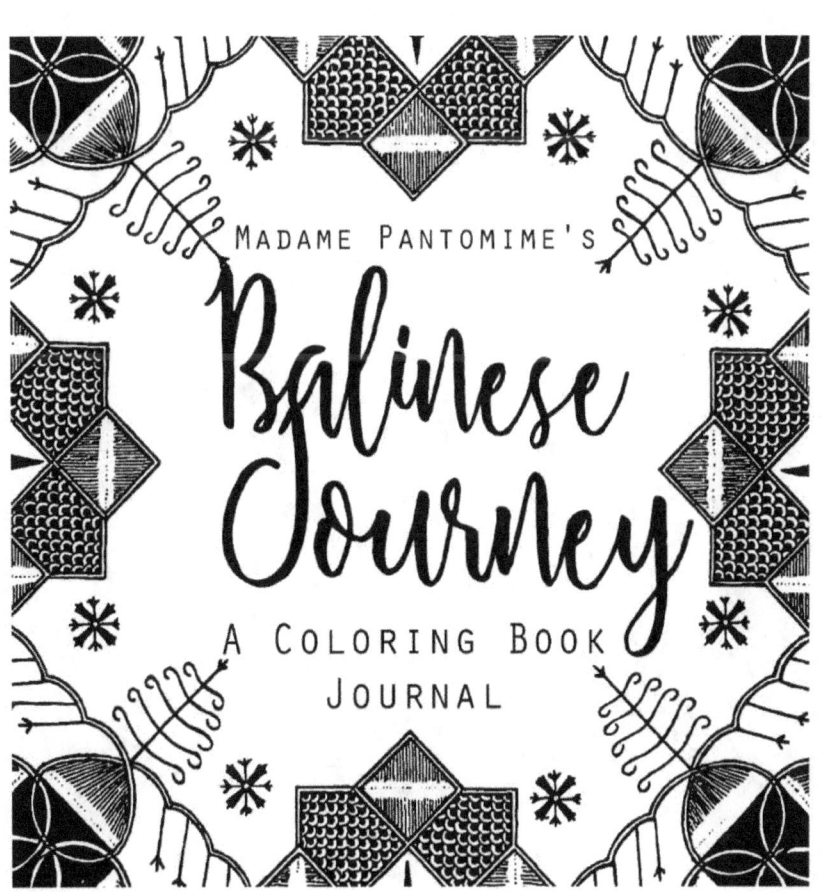

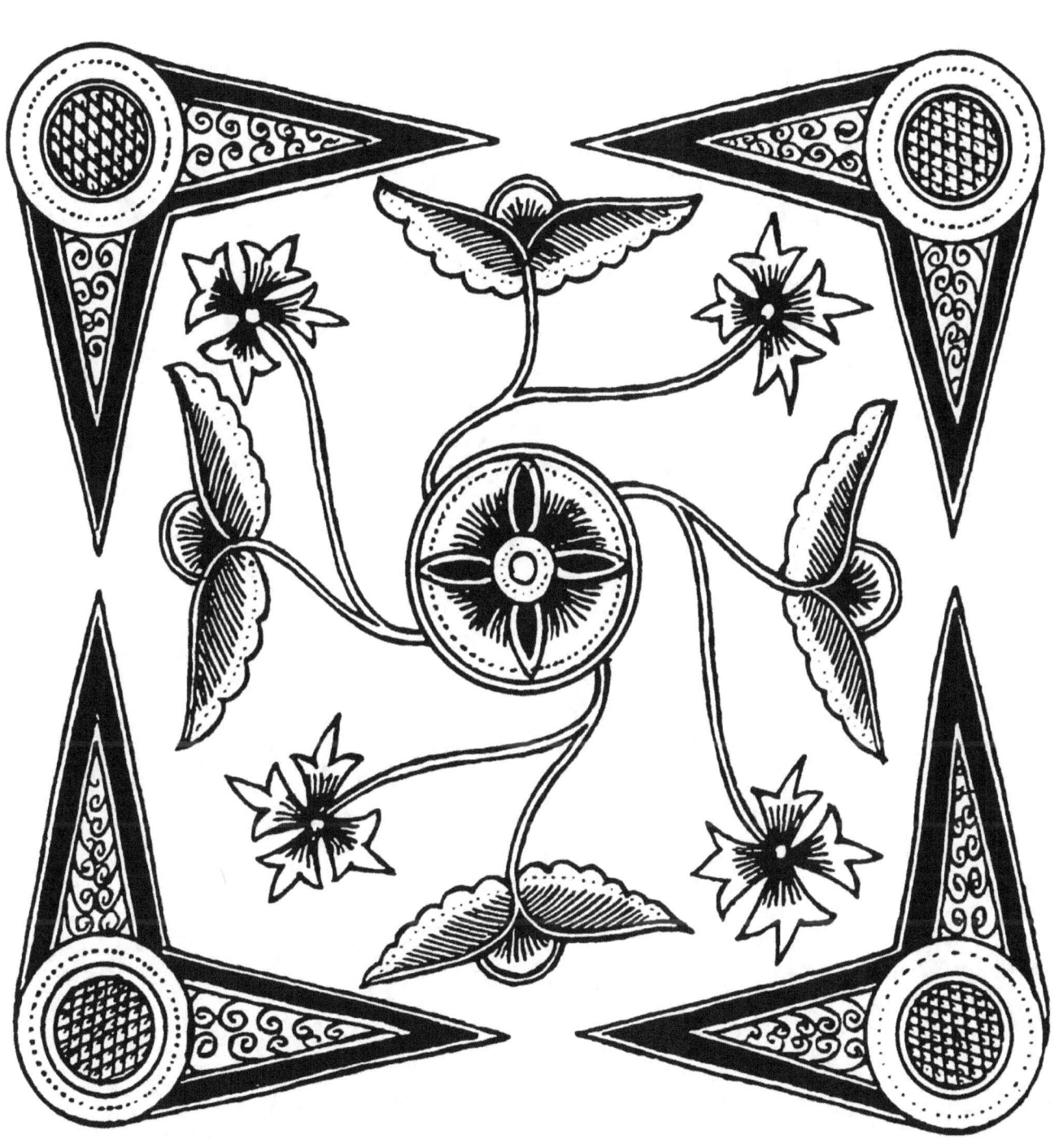

www.ingramcontent.com/pod-product-compliance
Lightning Source LLC
Chambersburg PA
CBHW081229280526
45787CB00006B/2581